CW00546214

Margaret Solis is one of the world's top psychics and mediums. Born in Scotland with *the gift of second sight,* she uses her exceptional gift and experience to help and guide people from all walks of life.

Having predicted for over 10,000 people over the course of her life—from housewives to top business men, from working class men and women to Lords and Ladies, from TV celebrities to film stars—she has accurately predicted their past, present and futures.

She continues to do so, and enjoys what she calls *"working with the light."*

Find out more about Margaret at:
www.margaretsolis.com

email: info@margaretsolis.com

Follow Margaret on:
FACEBOOK: @margaretsolispsychic
INSTAGRAM: @margaretsolispsychic

secret
psychic
stories
Volume 1

Margaret Solis

STARWiSH
BOOKS

STARWISH BOOKS is an imprint of SOLIS & solis ~ solisandsolis.com

STARWISH BOOKS

155 Kings Park Avenue, Glasgow, Scotland, UK, G44 4HZ

1

STARWISH BOOKS is an imprint of **SOLIS & solis** ~ solisandsolis.com

First published in 2021
Copyright © SOLIS & SOLIS 2021

A CIP catalogue record for this title is available from the British Library.

Paperback ISBN ~ 978-1-915040-01-5
Ebook ISBN ~ 978-1-915040-00-8

Some names and identifying details have been changed
to protect the privacy of individuals.

Every effort has been made to obtain the necessary permission with reference
to copyright material, both illustrative and quoted. We apologise for any
omissions in this respect and will be pleased to make the appropriate
acknowledgements in any future edition.

Typeset in 12 / 17 pt Athelas by www.TALISMAN.design

A prequel

to the

STARBRIGHT SERIES

contents

Preface 13

1. Sandra's Story 23

2. Andrew's Story 31

3. Ann's Story 33

4. Astrid's Story 35

5. Brenda's Story 39

6. Carla's Story 41

7. Deanna's Story 43

8. Dina's Story 45

9. Magda's Story 49

10. Fiona's Story 51

11. Gary's Story 53

12. Gillian's Story 55

13. Isabel's Story 57

14. James's Story 59

15. Jessica's Story 61

16. Jody's Story   64

17. Lynn's Story   66

18. Margaret's Story   68

19. Maria's Story   70

20. Marian's Story   72

21. Massimiliano's Story   75

22. Natalie K's Story   77

23. Nicola's Story   80

24. Rhonda's Story   82

25. Teresa's Story   85

26. Tony B's Story   86

27. Vivienne's Story   88

28. Yvonne's Story   90

29. Natalie's Story   92

30. Tony M's Story   95

Margaret Solis

Preface

*"All the world is made of faith, and trust,
and pixie dust."*

J.M. BARRIE, PETER PAN

Margaret Solis

Being psychic isn't recommended for the faint of heart. It can be a tough life in many ways, but it can also be a life full of wonderful and rewarding experiences when choosing to walk down destiny's path as a clairvoyant. Not that one has a real choice when you are truly psychic—if you're psychic, well... then you're psychic.

Yet, I feel fortunate to have been blessed with the *gift of second sight*, the gift of being psychic. Over the course of my lifetime this gift has opened a beautiful world of positive experiences for me, both on a personal as well as a professional level—from being able to see and experience psychic phenomena on a daily basis, to meeting wonderful people from all sorts of backgrounds, to travelling all over the country, and the world.

People have come to me for a reading from places that are close to home in Glasgow, and from places that are as far afield as the Far East, Russia, Australia, L.A, and New York and exotic, far-flung places such as The Bahamas, Dubai and Hawaii. Through my psychic work, I've helped, and made many lifelong friends with many amazing people. And that is one of the things that I absolutely love about doing what I do.

Over the years I have read thousands of people from all walks of life—from housewives to top business men, from working class men and women to Lords and Ladies, from TV celebrities to film stars.

I am often asked: "What's it like being psychic Margaret?"

As you can no doubt imagine, this is a difficult question to answer in itself. How do you describe the intangible, the invisible, the ethereal? It is a challenging thing to do for sure. I have however endeavoured to do so elsewhere, and in my other book—*'the good gift.'* In this book I write on a personal level and with as much clarity as I can, where I explain my experiences growing up with *the gift*, and how I see, hear, feel, taste, touch, experience... the things that I do as a psychic. Things that can be classed as out of bounds of the ordinary with regards to what are the accepted norms and boundaries of human perception.

But there is another way of explaining what this psychic 'stuff' is like... and that is by simply letting you explain it all in your own words. And where you tell your side of the story, so to speak.

So that's what I've done in this book.

The following pages contain a psychic compendium of stories, letters and messages, as written by you explaining how a psychic prediction (or indeed various predictions) came true. Or, how meeting me and experiencing the psychic side of life changed and impacted your own life in some way.

Some letters affirm how something that was said during a reading came true. Or, possibly, on reflection and afterthought, that what was said during the reading eventually made sense. The dots were connected as it were. When they had not at the actual time of the reading. In these cases people are often compelled to write to me describing what in actual fact was true, where they had been at a loss during the reading to place or confirm what I had said to them.

Others will write to me years after the reading took place, and where most (if not all) of my predictions have come true. If there are a few predictions yet to happen, then that person is usually seeking some kind of time-frame as to when the remaining predictions will be fulfilled and happen as predicted.

What I will say to this person is that you can't rush the future. I assure them that whatever the prediction is, it'll happen when it's supposed to happen.

A reading can take a lifetime for all the predictions

to come true. Or it can all happen in the space of a few weeks. Or even, and in some cases, over the course of a few days.

Each and every psychic reading is unique. The stories that follow in this book are written by you and are just as unique. And so, I leave the following words to you.

Margaret X

Margaret Solis
Glasgow, Scotland ~ July 2021

secret psychic stories *Volume 1*

Margaret Solis

Your stories...

*"Somewhere, something incredible
is waiting to be known."*

CARL SAGAN

Margaret Solis

• 1 •

SANDRA'S STORY

Scotland – June 2019

I MET MARGARET AT THE BEGINNING OF 1998 BY CHANCE, NOT DESIGN. A cousin in Glasgow had booked three afternoon appointments; the evening before she called, and I agreed to fill in for someone who couldn't make it. I had no clue even to Margaret's location as I left Edinburgh.

On arrival, we tossed a coin to sort out the order of readings. My cousin Chriss went off to do some shopping as she was last. A lady I'd never met, her friend Debbie, was first, so I sat in the hall of a pleasant house on Glasgow's south side. I was rather nervous as I had little experience of psychics.

I gave up scanning magazines, and concentrated on the future. I was at a real life crossroads, and wondered if some reassurance would emerge that I was on the right lines. I had just had a book accepted for publication but had no idea how it would be received. It was a highly controversial one, as I had named my own father—still alive at the time—as the person responsible for the abduction and murder of a young eleven year old, Moira Anderson.

She had disappeared from my hometown of Coatbridge when I was just eight, and what happened to her had remained a mystery for many years. I was convinced I had pinpointed the offender, but had gotten nowhere with the legal authorities in Scotland. As a last resort I had decided: *'The pen is mightier than the sword'*... Since my dad could sue the publishers and me, however, for defamation, it was a real risk. I worried about what lay ahead.

When Debbie eventually emerged, she looked a little shell-shocked, and whispered to me as Margaret popped upstairs briefly: "This lady is the real McCoy. I'm astonished, not only did she know my dad had recently passed, she saw me working on water. How could she possibly know I've just been offered a professional singing engagement on a cruise ship?? The letter's in my bag, only a handful of people are aware of the offer..."

"...but I'm going to go for it," she said.

"And she warned me of the Cruise Director making a pass at me too!"

"Wow!" I smiled, and started to feel surer that this

next hour was not about to be a waste of money.

Debbie sat next to me and frowned a little. "The only thing that Margaret said that made no sense to me at all was at the end. She said I'd a friend Sandra who's been in and out of police stations and written a book... well, I do have a friend of that name, but nothing like that's happened. Weird."

I gasped. Debbie registered astonishment on my face as Margaret descended her staircase.

"Goodness, it's me she's describing Debbie!" I gulped. "I'm that person."

Margaret, who had no names except my cousin's, paused at the foot of the stairs, puzzled.

"Hang on a moment," she said to Debbie. "Those last few messages I gave you are actually for her."

A very shrewd glance was cast over me. "It happens sometimes. You are Sandra, right??"

I agreed I was, and a somewhat gobsmacked Debbie nodded as I was ushered through to the room Margaret used for readings. It was very serene, with certainly nothing spooky about it, and I sat facing her across a small table draped with dark blue velvet material on which lay her Tarot cards.

Beautiful objects calmed me too, like a small Buddha she had with a smiling face, and she herself was the opposite of what some might expect of a clairvoyant, being open, friendly and humorous. She picked up her cards for me to shuffle, and then I picked up a writing pad. Taped recordings, we already had been warned, did not always turn out, so notes worked best to be on the safe side.

What an eyeopener of an hour it turned out to be.

For a stranger who had not even known some 24 hours before that she would be giving me a personal reading, Margaret made a whole raft of observations which I jotted down as she laid out various spreads of her cards and had me choose specific ones to turn over. As she rapidly interpreted what was going on in my life, her accuracy was startling on a number of levels. Yes, my mother was a Gemini, yes she was present, and her name was Mary, I confirmed. She'd passed over a few years ago. Not only did Margaret give a very clear description, she related a conversation my Mum was having so that I heard her messages to me.

"She had a really good laugh, you know, about a chair—basically she's in fits about it, but she says you'll know why." Margaret smiled and shrugged her shoulders. "What's that all about?"

"Oh. My. Word." I was overcome. It was a lightbulb moment. I knew with certainty that my mum was present. The woman opposite me, due to a rare gift, could both see and hear her.

"For months she had me phoning the Social Work Department about this awful chair they'd delivered to her home, she was out at the time and my uncle had accepted it," I stammered.

"She was raging with him—it was miles too big for her, with wings like those ones in old folk's homes, and she hated it with a passion, her feet couldn't even reach the ground! They kept promising they'd replace it, but they never did. She got totally fed up with them. Then, you won't credit this, but guess what happened?"

"Oh, I can believe what's coming next," guffawed Margaret. "She's laughing her head off here."

"The day of her funeral, we went to pick up my uncle and we all thought he was upset and crying. His shoulders were shaking, I explained, but in the limo, it turned out he was in stitches because the Social Work guy had just been to collect her throne as she called it, and deliver a replacement. "Chair for Mrs Gartshore!" The man was saying... My uncle said: "She won't be needing it now, son," and the poor guy's face was a picture when he heard she was being buried in an hour."

(This anecdote of a family event that really happened is so personal, no outsider could possibly have knowledge of it. I believe it was my mum's way of ensuring I knew this was no fake communication from someone purporting to be able to contact the 'Other Side.')

I saw Margaret had skills that could not be dismissed as coincidental or telling people what they wanted to hear. However, her other comment about the Chair was accurate in a more chilling way.

"Your mum tells me that where she is, she's happy that there is no chair for your father. He's called Alex, right? An Aquarian yes, I see. Well... because of what he has done, he will not have one."

And meeting this unique lady really clarified for me that I had done the right thing, and my mother was proud of my efforts to persist in getting justice for a small child whose parents had served a life sentence. I left hearing that Moira was a silent partner in everything I was going to do. I would set up a foundation to help those affected by sexual abuse. Margaret predicted a brooch with special powers and awards would come my way, including one from Prince Charles, a Scorpio and I would be at Buckingham Palace to receive it, so I should not be afraid of what was ahead. Everything pointed to success.

* * *

By 2000 I'd set up the Moira Anderson Foundation in memory of the little girl who had vanished. Two decades later, it has proved a lifeline to many individuals affected by child sexual abuse.

In 2005, I was voted Scotswoman of the Year by readers of Glasgow's Evening Times. Beforehand,

Margaret sent a message to say she had voted for me, but already knew I would win! I received the most beautiful Cairngorm amethyst brooch set in gold and diamonds in the shape of the Saltire, and it really does have a special energy. Then, the following year I was informed that I would be named in the Queen's Birthday Honours in the special year that was her eightieth.

Overwhelmed by this second honour, for services to Child Protection in Scotland, I decided to go to London at Christmas to receive it rather than at Holyrood in Edinburgh where I live. Our family flew down for the ceremony at the Palace, and fitted in shopping, a show and a meal at the Savoy.

As we entered the palace, my daughter and I headed for the loo and Lauren joked: "I bet you never thought you'd be putting on mascara in Buck House Mum! Looking forward to meeting H.M.?"

I recalled Margaret's prediction. "I have a funny feeling it will be Prince Charles somehow…"

Sure enough, we heard as we lined up that the Queen had hurt her back and most unusually, it was HRH who was filling in for her at this last investiture of the year.

"Should've made a bet with you guys that Margaret would be spot on," I told my husband and son.

And Margaret has continued to be uncannily spot on over the twenty years I have known her. She has become a dear friend though we may just see each other every eighteen months or so, and I value her advice. Margaret predicted my book about the case *Where There is Evil* would be a bestseller that would give me the means to launch the Foundation. She has always championed the work I undertook to support children and families affected by child sexual abuse. She has even warned me when any individual has tried to harm the charity, and has ensured messages from Moira are passed on to me. She has always maintained Moira wants to be found.

"Even if it doesn't happen, Sandra, Moira's legacy is amazing for a wee girl," she always stresses, "and it has come about because you took a deep breath—some would have run a mile!—and accepted the tough mission you were given. You found out exactly why you're here."

Inspiring in her own way, Margaret has helped countless people. I've never forgotten what she said about my mission in life. This quote from Mark Twain sums it up beautifully too:

'The two most important days of your life are the day you were born, and the day you find out why.'

Sandra Brown
Scotland ~ June 2019

· 2 ·

ANDREW'S STORY

Scotland – June 2019

Dear Margaret,

I AM SO GLAD I DROVE FROM EDINBURGH that September day four years ago to Kings Park, where I was welcomed by such a truly kind warm hearted spirit... of course, that is you Margaret.

Before I arrived for my reading, I was incredibly nervous, with no real understanding of how much a 'reading' with you would turn out to be, such a positive experience... so much of what you foresaw for me came to pass and materialised in my life!

The best description I can think of... is that you raised the curtain and shone a light onto, many ideas, events and thoughts I had not considered. The information you gleaned from me with your intuitive gift helped me edit and craft my life in a more wise and positive way.

The way you unfolded the map of the previously unknown, without any doubt, has turned out to be a treasured helping hand in my life.

Warmest gratitude,

Andrew Douglas Moore
Scotland ~ June 2019

• 3 •

ANN'S STORY

Scotland ~ August 2019

YOU TOLD ME ON MY FIRST VISIT TO SEE YOU that someone's teeth were coming out, this was before you even knew I had kids. My daughters tooth came out that night.

You told me that my daughter: "didn't like to get her hands dirty."

TRUE! She's the laziest person I know.

You told me my son would be into martial arts, kickboxing etc. He was about 10 / 12yrs old and not at all interested in any kind of sport. He didn't ever play sports games on his consoles—he was a skinny and introverted geek. I was sure you had got this very wrong. But no. Ross in now 27 yrs old, gym buff, does mixed martial arts and won his first cage fight. The whole family are shocked at his change in hobbies! You were right again!!

You said my dad was coming back over from Africa—how you knew he even lived there was a shock. He never comes over and he'd already made a brief visit so I wasn't really sure about that information. However, when I left your house and got into my car my sister-in-law called me to say that: "my dad was coming over from Africa in a few weeks."

SHOCK! And you were right, he didn't visit any of us. He went to London and made lame excuses of why he had no need to come up to Scotland!

You told me to look out for a red-headed woman as she would cause me harm. I had a few red-headed ladies in my friends at work circle but no one that bad. Then I met a woman who was charming and lovely. I never once suspected her of being this person you warned me about. She turned out to be the most vicious, verminous woman I have ever met. She caused trouble from here to the US, her name is ******** ********* (I really wish you could use her name!) she made my life hell, and I soon found that I wasn't the only one.

She was a complete liar, and user, AND... she had bright red dyed hair! I should have known—LOL!

Ann Mitchell
Scotland ~ August 2019

• 4 •

ASTRID'S STORY

Spain ~ August 2019

Dear Margaret,

AROUND 2002 I HAD MY FIRST EVER SESSION WITH YOU. I had just moved to Spain and I tried to get used to the British accent of the people living here. There was no Skype, just a normal landline back then, and I could hardly follow what you said during my phone reading due to your Scottish accent.

I remember that you asked me if I lost a child, or had had an abortion, as you saw no child in my life. Your question irritated me so I didn't give this session too much attention as at that time my little girl was playing downstairs.

You suggested to prepare myself and put some money aside as you saw lots of paperwork and legal stuff coming related to my partner, I was convinced that it was not about me. Back then I did not give your words too much importance. But after what happened some years later, I certainly do now...

-- In 2007 my partner sued me twice in two different countries and I never saw my child again (parental alienation) even though I was fighting like a lioness.

-- In 2012 I was told that I would buy an apartment, and I did.

Last November I had another psychic reading with you and was told that I am going to go to a place I always wanted to go. You were right as I travelled to America last December to join the biggest Tony Robbins event.

I have not been caught out for an intervention as you predicted but it can still happen one day, who knows.

You've always talked about a connection to video, film, radio and I could not relate to that. Today I can though, as this year I joined a Facebook group where I needed to 'Go live' for a 30 day-challenge. I still do it on my own page now because I enjoy doing it, specially because I feel supported now.

During a reading, you will also call out names that are impossible for anyone to know. You point out illnesses and /or weaknesses that blow me away. And, you also don't mince your words when asked about death.

The space of time is not necessarily as predicted, but you and the Universe seem to be great friends.

I have been told beautiful things are to come now, and I am desperately and patiently waiting for it to become reality. I could reconcile with my daughter on a friendship level and I already should be married with the love of my life, besides moving into a new home this year. I am clueless but hopeful as it would break this unhealthy eleven year circle. And of course I would love the fact that you are right regarding my financial success.

Whenever I am in despair I take out all those papers from the readings with you and I go through them. It automatically gives me peace, hope and faith knowing that many things you said happened to be true.

With love and appreciation,

Astrid Noebauer
Spain ~ August 2019

• 5 •

BRENDA'S STORY

Spain ~ August 2019

Hi Margaret,

I'VE BEEN COMING TO SEE YOU for readings on a regular basis for over twenty years, and you've given me such amazing advice about my future and accurately predicted so many wonderful things. Here are a few...

You said I would have a self-employed business and be extremely successful, working and living in Spain... I got into selling real estate in the Caribbean after many miserable years as a Pharmaceutical Representative.

You predicted that I would visit, St Lucia, Dominican Republic, Barbados and would successfully sell property in all these countries and I did. I also bought a holiday apartment in Spain and only thought I would commute for holidays but things changed in my life and circumstances meant that I lived happily in Spain for a number of years and sold real estate in the Caribbean.

You told me my husband was cheating with two different women and that was also true. One of them had two daughters and you also told me she had lost a son. Accurate again!

You said my husband's health would be bad and he had diabetes. He was diagnosed with diabetes a few months later.

I remember bumping into you in Glasgow years ago and my son was with me. Straight out you said he would be a pilot. A few years later he went to flying school in Florida.

During my reading you always tell me countries I'm going to live in. In 2017 you said I would go to Dubai. Once again my circumstances changed and I was offered a job selling real estate in Dubai and I lived there for a while.

I've been doing Airbnb this year. And as you said the business would be good, although I would make a few mistakes. I did make a few mistakes with my listing but that's all been resolved now. You said I would move to my flat at the beach because the Airbnb income would allow me to do that. I move back there in the next few months.

You predicted my son's partner would have a baby boy. And she did last year.

The last reading I had from you had a message from my Aunt and cousin who had both recently passed. They wanted to let me know they were fine. You knew how they had died and that gave me confidence that it was actually them.

You also told me that my son would separate from his partner and sadly that's what's happened.

Brenda McAlister
Scotland ~ August 2019

• 6 •

CARLA'S STORY

Scotland ~ August 2019

I ALWAYS TURN TO MARGARET in times of turmoil. And I always feel calmer after talking with her.

I was struggling to have a baby. She told me it was definitely happening. And soon. I was about to do IVF which I didn't tell her. It failed. I called her again and she told me it was definitely happening and she saw two babies. Twins.

My second IVF was successful. It was twins, but I lost one in early stages of pregnancy.

She had also told my mum two years previously that she would have seven grandchildren. She already had six and we clung onto the hope that maybe the seventh would be mine. It was!!

She is no nonsense. Doesn't sugar coat anything but you come away feeling clearer, calmer and hopeful.

She's always my go-to. A very special woman with a wonderful gift.

Carla
Scotland ~ August 2019

• 7 •

D E A N N A ' S   S T O R Y

Los Angeles, California – July 2019

Dear Margaret,

I WAS HIGHLY RECOMMENDED to your services approximately fifteen years ago. I recall walking through the door and before I even sat down you had said...

"You are married."
...Yes!

"You have two kids."
...Yes!

"A son and a daughter."
...Yes!

"Hello, I am Margaret come take a seat."

Since then I have had the pleasure of meeting with you numerous times. I have referred many friends, colleagues and family members to you as well whom have also been very pleased. Additionally, I have done readings with you online, over the phone and in person. I have found these readings to be very informative, detailed and accurate.

I take notes at each appointment and refer back to them often to verify certain dates, names and events. Some of the information during the readings were from past events which provided confirmation and accuracy. Many of the readings have also provided current events, as well as future.

Some of my favorite experiences have included information and messages from loved ones that have passed away, human and animal. Each time something occurs, which you have predicted, we call that a *'Margaretism.'* :)

Deanna
Los Angeles, California ~ July 2019

• 8 •

DINA'S STORY

Los Angeles, California ~ August 2019

MARGARET SOLIS HAS TOUCHED MY LIFE IN SO MANY WAYS that limiting my story to something relatively short will be nearly impossible.

To frame my experience with her it would be best to tell about my very first meeting, in which I am able to confirm she had no way of knowing who I was, or anything about my life.

One day a friend of a friend mentioned Margaret to me and I said I had always wanted to visit someone like her and asked to have the number where I could reach her. As a skeptic, I limited my conversation to giving my first name and the setting of the appointment. So many incredible discoveries came from that first meeting and, for me, what was so special was that I learned Margaret is able to talk about the past, present, and future. She is also able to communicate with loved ones who have passed, and she does so in a remarkable manner.

This first story happened during my first reading with her... Margaret mentioned to me that she was hearing from my grandfather (my mom's dad) and that he wanted to let me know to tell my mom that she gave him the namesake she wanted to honor him with... I argued with Margaret because as the story went, my mom wanted to honor her father with a grandchild named after him but he passed away before she could.

I was born 8 ½ months before he died and my mom was not able to name me John since I was a girl. Margaret and I argued back and forth until she said:

"Your grandfather is telling me that the baby your mom miscarried right before he died was a boy, and John has been with him this entire time!"

Well of course I burst into tears, as I did know my mom did miscarry 8 months after I was born and the baby was nearly 5 months old... this was the 1960's so gender reveals were not as advanced as today. I knew in that moment that Margaret had a gift beyond anything I had encountered in my life and certainly one I was not able to fully understand. Hearing this and everything else she told me in that session brought me an amazing sense of peace and filled me with an energy that comes from knowing and feeling a part of our beautiful universe.

Another situation was when I was going through a divorce (Margaret did see that coming...). Margaret saw the outcome and was able to give me extreme detail in terms of how long it would take and specifics regarding the judges on my case. What was amazing was that she was also able to see that I needed to change my attorney. Subsequently I received a call from a friend who worked for my previous attorney who shared with me that my attorney at the time had made a financial deal with my estranged husband, and that I should leave him as soon as possible... a confirmation of what Margaret had just told me!

There are so many on point stories I could tell, but I will end with this final one that still amazes me! I was on the phone with Margaret when she interrupted me and asked who the Capricorn man with the fatal illness was...? I replied my brother's father in-law. She told me she was talking with him and that he wanted me to tell everyone that he was ok and happy, and to not worry.

I told her: "Margaret, this is nonsense he is alive. I just spoke with my brother and actually this man had just returned from the doctor and was doing okay."

Margaret explained that sometimes the spirit leaves the body a few days prior to the actual physical death. That was a Wednesday and of course I called my brother right after my conversation with Margaret and he said I was crazy for believing such a thing. Two days later, at 11am on that Friday, my brother called me and he was crying that Margaret had been correct and that his father-in-law had just passed.

This man who we all loved was battling lung cancer... but on that day he died from a massive heart attack.

While some may feel this story is tragic, I can confirm that it was absolutely beautiful in that Margaret was able to share with our family a message of love from our loved one and to let us all know the answer to what people want to know... that after this life our loved ones are happy and at peace!

Thank you Margaret you are a true blessing in my life!

Dina
Los Angeles, California ~ August 2019

• 9 •

MAGDA'S STORY

Glasgow, Scotland ~ August 2019

I FIRST MET MARGARET IN 1989, when she visited the island I lived on, for holidays. I was sixteen years old then and did not know what a clairvoyant and psychic was. I had no idea what the tarot cards were either.

Margaret did a reading for a family member of mine, who was astonished with what they were told. I still remember looking at her with awe.

The years passed by and it was my wish that she did a reading for me. I visited Glasgow for holidays and my wish came true. I could not believe what I was told. She had the ability to see scenes. I could not believe I would live in the exact same scene Margaret had recently described to me.

Margaret was talking to me as a friend and giving

me precious advice as well. I had such a huge issue back then and when she told me it would be solved, I prayed inside me that her words would become true. And they did! Then she became my good fairy.

I visited her again when I had work issues and again her words became true. I could not believe things happened, as I was told, less than a month later.

The weird thing is that every time I have had a reading with Margaret, I have burst into tears after it. I cannot explain this. It's as if Margaret takes away all the bad energy from me and fills me with optimism and good energy. I recommended Margaret to a few of my friends who were amazed with her predictions. Margaret's charisma is a phenomenon.

As life is unpredictable, I now live in Glasgow as well and glad Margaret is near for readings. I am looking forward to visiting her again soon.

Magda
Glasgow, Scotland ~ August 2019

• 1 0 •

FIONA'S STORY

Scotland ~ June 2019

Dear Margaret,

I CAME FOR A READING WITH YOU IN JANUARY 2009 and I vividly remember it, as what you predicted was about my eldest son, Jamie. You always say to write everything down at the beginning of the reading and when you came out with this prediction I was somewhat startled!

You said my son, that was into music, would be on the front page of a newspaper, and also there would be a double page spread inside with him featured.

I was alarmed at first as I thought he may do something wrong or something may happen to him, but you assured me this wouldn't be the case.

Three months later, as you predicted...

...he was in the newspaper!

There was an article written about Stow College and he was photographed—he was the one with the whacky hair and glasses, on the front page of the Evening Times and in the centre pages. Plus, they interviewed him too!

Spot on Margaret!

Fiona Brennan
Scotland ~ June 2019

· 11 ·

GARY'S STORY

Scotland - August 2019

Dear Maggie,

FIRST OF ALL I JUST WANT TO START THIS BY SAYING *thank you* for:

1. Saving my life *(literally!)*
2. Impacting my life in such a positive way

Before I came to see you, I can honestly say I was a skeptic.

Looking back, before meeting you I was living in a cycle where I thought I was living a normal life. A problem I had but never really addressed was that I was taking recreational drugs in the majority of social situations I would find myself in.

Because it's so normalised, I genuinely didn't think I had an issue and didn't see how it was negatively impacting my life. After meeting you and processing the predictions from the cards that unfolded, seeing my likely death before my very eyes really hit home.

The cards showed that if I were to keep living this lifestyle, I would die within the next three months. You asked me to call you in July so you knew I was ok. And I did.

Now I am completely drug free, business is booming, my head is screwed on and I know it's exactly where I am heading in life.

I believe you are truly gifted, and am so grateful for the path you have led me on. For this, I will be forever be in your debt. You changed my life.

Thank you, from the bottom of my heart.

Gary Greenhill
Scotland ~ August 2019

· 1 2 ·

GILLIAN'S STORY

Scotland – August 2019

I HAD A READING FROM YOU MARGARET IN 2010 and I also met yourself at the Girl's Day Out show at the SEC in Glasgow. I can't remember if this was before, or after, my actual reading. However, you changed my life, and for the better.

I was in a very bad relationship. And from the first moment we actually met you told me to leave and that I didn't know the extent of this man's lies.

I was never abused or anything like that, but this man was a liar and was leading a double life.

I remember the day... and I walked away saying: "aye. whatever...

But, oh... my... god!...

It all started to unravel, and I very quickly realised you were right!

You also told me I was going to go through a health issue that would be very difficult for everyone involved but it would all turn out fine. I haven't come across this as yet, but I see how this can happen and I am working on different herbal ways of life to possibly prevent this.

The biggest thing you told me was I was going to meet my knight in shining armour and I was going to have a child before the age of 31. And yes, this happened, and has changed my life for the better in so many ways.

I met Al in May 2010. We didn't get together until end of July due to me having trust issues from the last idiot!!! We had our son in 2013.

I had blinkers on before my reading and you have helped to guide me in the right direction so I want to say thank you and that I will be back to get another reading. And soon.

Gillian Proudfoot
Glasgow, Scotland ~ August 2019

• 1 3 •

ISABEL'S STORY

Los Angeles. California – August 2019

WHAT A GIFT MARGARET SOLIS HAS BEEN IN MY LIFE. I went to see her at a friend's house the first time over ten years ago in a time of great change in my life. That first reading left me feeling empowered, light and confident.

Every single piece of information that came through her in that reading, and in every reading since, has come to fruition. And if the predictions haven't happened yet, I know it's just a matter of time before they do.

The accuracy of Margaret's readings is just remarkable. I have seen a lot of very talented psychics, mystics and shamans in my life and Margaret is by far the best. She delivers the information clearly, and connects the dots.

Her readings are so impactful because they are pure,

and from a source meant to reach us as we are. Her work has helped and will continue to help so many.

Big things like my relationship & marriage, children, jobs, births, deaths, as well as moves and projects as well small things like passport renewals, needed Doctor's appointments and vacations to be taken with my family, etc—it has all come through. All have helped me from easing anxiety to helping me organize logistically in order to get something done.

I don't see a therapist but having a session with Margaret a couple times a year has been an amazing way to receive guidance, support, and affirmation.

We all have moments in which we feel the need to ask questions, or to work out a problem, talk things through with someone that has a deep connection to spirit other than ourselves. I call Margaret my Auntie Margaret because that is the bond and friendship we have built over the years. She is funny, straightforward and a lovely woman I am proud to know.

I always leave our sessions feeling empowered, inspired and connected to my mission here on earth. Thank you Margaret for sharing your gifts with the world. I am so grateful you are in my life.

Love you,

Isabel Barreto
Los Angeles, California ~ August 2019

· 1 4 ·

J A M E S ' S   S T O R Y

Scotland ~ August 2019

I CAME TO YOU THREE YEARS AGO
LOOKING FOR GUIDANCE when I was still high on
drugs and wasting my life to gambling addiction.

You told me not to worry as I would get clean. I am
now two years clean and sober from drugs and gambling.

You told me I would shoot for the stars and be
surrounded by celebrities of all kinds. I now have one of
the biggest podcasts in the UK, interviewing the biggest
names.

And you also told me you seen my name would be up
in lights and three years later you were at my screening
of my homeless documentary—with my name in lights!

You told me I would be surrounded with loads
of cameras and now I am doing my podcasts and
documentaries.

You told me I would meet my future wife at 35.

I have just turned 35 and so I'm now waiting for this one :)

James English
Scotland ~ August 2019

• 1 5 •

JESSICA'S STORY

Glasgow, Scotland ~ June 2019

HI MY NAME IS JESSICA JAYASINGHA and I'm from Sri Lanka. I live in Glasgow's south side and I beautify your nails.

I first met Margaret Solis in 2004 in a Glasgow West End shop that I worked in at the time.

One day I was at work and a blonde lady walks into the shop and says pointing at me: "I want this girl to do the nails on my feet."

Since that day when I first met her, she would tell me so many things that would happen in my life which would eventually come true...

I.   I would one day marry a man from another country.

2. I would own my own shop.

But I had never had a reading at that point. Every time she came to the shop she amazed me with the things she told about life stuff. She actually told me so many things about my childhood without me telling her anything about myself.

In 2008, after my father's death, for some reason I thought about Margaret, as I had no one to talk to at the time. Soon after I called her and she asked me to come to her house that same Tuesday night. Then, when I first walked into her reading room all the lights flickered and dimmed up and down. She right away told me I lost someone close to me (she never knew my dad had passed away as she was on holiday at the time it happened).

The reading Margaret gave me that day gave me comfort to my grieving heart. And scarily, she told me a few things about my dad that I had never talked to anyone about.

As time passed and I began to see her more and more often. We became such good friends, and I feel she has always cared so much about me.

Now, years later, I have my own shop—as Margaret told me I would—and I've called it *'Nails Jessi.'*

Any time she visits me at the shop she always gives me good vibes and good positive thoughts. She pushes me to do the best I can. It makes me think that Margaret is my healing person. Personally, it's always worked for me and it helps me to this day to talk to her.

As Margaret constantly reassures me, she says I've done so well, and she was spot on so many personal situations in her readings.

Also, as some of my clients know, she gets her nails done at my shop. They whisper (asking me) is she magical, and is she really psychic, and how does she know the stuff she knows? I just smile and say that she's all of that and more, and her name is Margaret Solis.

I'm so proud to be her wee friend, and I'm blessed to have her as the longest and most loyal client in my nails career.

Because I chose Margaret, she's always been so kind to me. And you know that I feel like she can read my mind as well. She is constantly amazing me with her magic words, and predictions!

Love from wee Jessi x

Jessica Jayasingha
Glasgow, Scotland ~ June 2019

• 16 •

JODY'S STORY

Glasgow, Scotland ~ June 2019

———

THE FIRST TIME I went for a reading with Margaret, I was so, so nervous.

Loads of different things had happened in my life— my mother and father had passed and I was a mess with grief. A friend had been diagnosed with cancer. And I was up in the air with work.

As soon as I sat down with Margaret a calm came over me. She asked me to pick out three cards, and literally, my life perception changed at that moment!!

She gave me a telling off for not believing in myself. My parents came through to say they loved me and were proud and 5 pences would be the sign that they were with me. I now find them everywhere.

My friend's cancer diagnosis came up with a lucky 7 card. True to form, 7 months later, they got the all clear.

As for work, I'm now running my own successful business.

I can't understand how different my life is now from when I first went to see Margaret for a reading.

Worlds apart… amazing!

Jody Ciplinski
Glasgow, Scotland ~ June 2019

• 1 7 •

LYNN'S STORY

Scotland – August 2019

Hi Margaret,

I JUST WANT TO THANK YOU AGAIN.

I've had two readings with yourself and each brought so much clarity, healing and hope to me.

Before one reading in particular I was filled with self-doubt on a certain situation occurring in my life. During my reading with you this was addressed in great detail and I felt a sense of ease and now trust my own intuition more than ever.

You've empowered me to live my truth and go after my dreams.

You and your gift are a blessing and I'm grateful we got a chance to meet.

Much love & light,
Lynn x

Lynn Kellow
Scotland ~ August 2019

· 1 8 ·

MARGARET'S STORY

Scotland – June 2019

I FIRST MET MARGARET THROUGH A FRIEND who knew I was going through a bad time at home. I felt so alone and lost.

I'm an artist and painter, so he suggested I do a portrait of Margaret's choice in exchange for a reading, which she agreed to.

Margaret predicted many things that have come true...

I was to be widowed within a six. It was six months to the day he died after my visit to see Margaret.

I would also be signing a lot of papers. Lawyers would be involved. But the fight would make me a stronger person and I would move on and life would be good again. I would make new friends and my art work would flourish. I would also be moving house.

And yes life is getting better. I'm going to move, but only when I am ready. I'm doing things I never thought possible with my art and I'm determined never to go down again.

My confidence is coming back — I'm first on the dance floor and learning to live again, life is good.

Thank you Margaret Solis. X

Margaret Strang
Scotland ~ June 2019

• 19 •

MARIA'S STORY

California, USA ~ August 2019

MY NAME IS MARIA USITALO AND I FIRST MET MARGARET IN 2011.

I was born and raised with catholic family values, therefore I never had a psychic reading in my life. But someone introduced me to Margaret, and I never will regret having her do a psychic reading for me.

She told me things only I and God knew.

She warned me about others and told me at the time of the reading to write things down, and that although they may seem irrelevant at the moment, they would make sense in the future. And boy was she right. I have everything written down and when I go back and read my notes... WOW!!!

From the selling of my house, to new job opportunities, to family, to legal matters. If anyone would've told me how accurate Margaret is, I would never have believed it.

And, it's all still happening—my son did live in Canada, he's now back in California. The name that reappeared so often and in my mind since you told me during my reading, ended up being my grandson. Without me having anything to do so and many other things, I'm now only waiting for that man of my dreams. Margaret saw him in my reading and everything has been spot on so far, so I'm not worried. It will happen.

Margaret, you change my way of seeing things, and in a very positive way ever since that very first day that I met you. And for that, I'm forever thankful for your existence.

Sincerely yours truly,

Maria Usitalo
California ~ August 2019

• 2 0 •

MARIAN'S STORY

Scotland ~ August 2019

I HAD THE PLEASURE OF MEETING
MARGARET SOME YEARS AGO.
I had a reading and I tried to make whatever she
was saying fit into my interpretation of what I thought
it meant. This was a mistake. Things are never literal
and exact—not in any psychic reading would this be the
case.

I took the paper from the reading, stuck it in a
drawer and forgot all about it, two years later I found it
and read it again—I was astonished. It all made sense
but not in the way I had thought about it in the moment
of the reading.

Having had a few more readings over the years, I
now have a back catalogue of instances where Margaret
has given me information on things that she could not

know in advance and she was correct on her reading.

Margaret has informed me about boyfriends—in one instance—I would be the first girlfriend of TEN!—and, unfortunately for me, I was. The important information was, that she predicted this before I had even met him. It didn't change the experience for me as these were my choices and, of course, my life. Again I realised this in retrospect when I re-read the notes from my reading years later. Margaret had described him, gave me what he had trained in, and even how many children he had.

Margaret informed me about new jobs, new cars—I had a fender bender that she knew about, meeting new people, the countries I was travelling to in advance of going. Families, births and good wishes from past family members with messages that would be information that only they would know She gave me their names and described some of their interests or passions which they still had.

She has accurately predicted about my family—passing of exams, getting new jobs, partners, moving houses, birth of babies etc . She would even also tell me the month these changes would happen and this was to me all very spooky, and very correct. Recently, I bought lots of shoes in the sales—Margaret asked me "Why can I see lots of shoes?"—l laughed.

Margaret you are a lovely person—your gift is special and it is fantastic that you share it with us. Thank you.

Passing on warmth and love, and sometimes passing on messages from our families. For me I am glad that I met you and hope you continue on your journey, as I am sure that is what you were sent to do in the world.

For me—Margaret, you allowed me to see, that in life, we are only in a moment in time. Things change in all sorts of ways and to remember that change is constant—enjoy the good moments and work through the bad, remember that bad moments will pass and all experience is life learning, always to have hope, believe in karma and be your best self, send love and kindness to all people and do not expect anything back from doing so, as we are all at different stages in our journey. Always look forward to the next chapter, and in order for a new chapter to start, an old one must end.

I hope you continue—the world needs you and you make a difference.

Sending you lots of love, best wishes and happiness.

Marian Byrne
Scotland ~ August 2019

• 2 1 •

MASSIMILIANO'S STORY

London, UK – June 2019

MY NAME IS MASSIMILIANO VICCARDI, I'm an Italian and I live in London.

I first met Margaret Solis for a reading in London and I remember two things that she specifically said to me...

I asked about my mother and if she would be able to sell my grandmother's flat. Margaret gave me the exact date that the sale of the property actually happened on. My mother received a phone call from the estate agent to say that the house was sold, on that date!

The other thing that she said was: "I can see a close friend of yours, a couple who are married... I see a name John... they will divorce."

I only knew one John who was my friend. We were very close friends, and despite everything was going kind of well with his wife, they suddenly divorced.

That is what I remember about my reading with Margaret Solis.

Massimiliano Viccardi
London, UK ~ June 2019

• 2 2 •

NATALIE K'S STORY

Scotland ~ June 2019

Dear Margaret,

I WILL NEVER, EVER, FORGET MY FIRST READING WITH YOU. A friend of mine had told me that I should come and see you as my love life was going nowhere. I had been seeing a boy I was madly in love with, but didn't seem to be reciprocated, so I wanted a reading in the hope that this was the boy I would marry. I think I was 18 at the time, so this is 37 years ago. It is still as clear as the day I met you.

The reading was great and it all seemed that things were looking hopeful and when you asked me if I had any questions I said yes, will I get married soon. You looked at me and said:

"Yes, you will be married within 6 months but not to him."

"In fact you haven't met him yet."

At that time I thought that was crazy and was actually quite angry when I left.

6 months later I was married to another guy! I went back to tell you that unbelievably you were right and I was so happy. You looked at me and shook your head and said:

"I'm really sorry but it is not going to last."

I don't think it was 6 months before we filed for divorce, not because I didn't love him but he was a Walter Mitty character and again you were spot on.

You also described the flat I was going to move into and the trees outside it which I didn't realise until I had moved in and one day I was standing across from it and thought... oh my God, Margaret described this to a tree!

My sister was told by you from the age of 18 that she would be moving to America. We both laughed at that as we have great aunts there, but certainly no one that would make her move. You also told her she would marry someone she already knew. Years later she was contacted by an old friend who asked if he could meet her. She hadn't seen him since she was 14 as he had moved away. Where had he moved to? America. (I'm laughing as I write this :)

Where is she now? America... happily married and with 2 kids. And I'm sure you predicted both would be boys too.

You are one in a million. You can, and do, see the future!

Love Natalie x

Natalie King
Scotland ~ June 2019

• 2 3 •

NICOLA'S STORY

Glasgow, Scotland ~ June 2019

———

I HAVE BEEN TO MARGARET SOLIS about four times over the years and each time I go my future still is the exact same. However, she always goes into more detail each time.

Everything she has told me is now being revealed before my eyes. I first went to her in my early 20s when I was really unlucky in relationships and she made me realise that I kept looking for the same relationship as my parents, but that my future would be different. She was so right!

She said I would travel lots and be around music and art. She said America, Spain, and could see me living in London in the future and I'd be very happy there.

I went to America and taught in a Summer Camp, I moved to Madrid and taught there for six months, lived in Abu Dhabi for two years teaching & for the last two years I now live in Essex, near London. So she was right with all her predictions.

She said the "name David" would be my perfect match and that he would have an accent. She said this when I was in my early 20s. Margaret said that I would meet my perfect match around my 30s and that from 35-40 I'll have had two kids; one boy and then a girl and get married during this time.

I'm 36 now, we have just bought a house and have a little boy due in September. So will need to see if I have a girl next too and get married.

With my career, she said that children were always going to be around me, (I'm a teacher), and that I would be promoted in the future and could see music and art around me. Now at the age of 36, I am leader of Arts in the school and have been a primary teacher for the last 14 years.

Margaret has a real gift and amazing insight and I thoroughly enjoy getting a reading every time I go to see her.

Nicola
Glasgow, Scotland ~ June 2019

• 2 4 •

RHONDA'S STORY

Scotland ~ June 2019

OVER THE YEARS I have had many readings from Margaret Solis and many predictions have come true.

I was encouraged by Margaret to go back and study as a mature student. She told me to believe in myself and make my own life work. So I enrolled at a local college. I was a terrible worrier, and hated the thought of failing, but Margaret said to me reach for the moon and fall amongst the stars. Anyway, I graduated in 2010 with Business Management. All my grades were B passes. I was so delighted after having left school at sixteen with virtually no qualifications.

A few years later Margaret said I was a little lost in life and didn't know where I was going. I was told my health problems would go away which puzzled me. I had no idea I was about to contract pneumonia and be very unwell for over the course of two years.

Margaret said she could see me owning my own business but I would firstly do training courses and gain more certificates. She said: "use your transferable skills to succeed." She mentioned a school run for children, which puzzled me as my children had completed their schooling.

Time passed, and I kept trying out different job roles but never settled. I knew I could do so much better and that I had to push on. I took Margaret's advice and a huge risk of leaving my job as a supervisor in a 5 star Pet Hotel & Spa and decided to train as a dog groomer. I virtually lived on fresh air. Having been a qualified hairdresser I felt I had an advantage over the other students. The course included Canine First Aid and a Dog Behavioural Course. I continued to work at the Training Academy for six months to get more experience, hoping I would secure a paid job. But in the end I made the decision to start my own business.

I contacted my local council and they arranged a visit to my home, within a few days I had my license for Dog Grooming and home boarding. I'm now the proud owner of Barks & Bubbles Pet Services Alloway. Since I opened in June I have worked non-stop and have never been happier, or more in control of my life.

I also have been granted my PVG for vulnerable adults & children, which will allow me to help out with my husband's business Ayr2B Taxis. He does school runs for children with learning disabilities and on occasions will require my help as a child minder.

I have so much to thank Margaret for, she is kind, caring, encouraging and was there for me when I had no one. I love her to the moon and back. She's one in a million.

Thank you Margaret, and please keep helping others through your wonderful work.

Lots of love,

Rhonda Patrick
Scotland ~ June 2019

• 2 5 •

T E R E S A ' S   S T O R Y

Scotland ~ August 2019

M A R G A R E T ' S   P R E D I C T I O N S have always been absolutely impressive.

I have been a regular client since 2000. I live in Barcelona and I met Margaret here in my city when she came here to visit family and friends.

I now come to her in Glasgow for my readings or through Skype.

I like to contrast her readings with my goals, ambitions and life circumstances.

And she always hits her predictions with an impressive level of detail.

Teresa Granado
Barcelona ~ August 2019

· 2 6 ·

T O N Y   B ' S   S T O R Y

Scotland ~ June 2019

—

M A R G A R E T ' S   G I F T   A S   A   C L A I R V O Y A N T has confounded me on numerous occasions.

From our first meeting, Margaret had a remarkable insight into who I was, who my parents were and an uncanny knowledge of my destiny. Even now, I still refer to notes from our two sittings, only to discover her predictions continue to have significant relevance in my life.

Margaret is a consummate professional and an extremely talented and gifted human being.

If one's soul is open to Margaret's gift, you will discover some special insights into many aspects of your current journey on this earth.

Tony Bond
Scotland ~ June 2019

• 27 •

VIVIENNE'S STORY

Glasgow, Scotland ~ August 2019

Dear Margaret,

I BELIEVE MY FIRST READING WITH YOU WAS IN 1999. You made me feel so welcome and I felt as if I was visiting a close friend rather than a stranger. I have continued to come to you for readings over the years simply because they are spookily accurate and I have always had a fascination for tarot cards. This in part is due to my Gran, who liked to read the tarot. I feel I have also always been very instinctive about situations and naturally curious about psychic predictions.

On my first psychic reading with you I remember you advised me to write everything down and I'm so glad I did! I have referred to these notes often over the years.

Some names and predicted events materialised

quickly in my life and at first I was tempted to put it down to coincidence. But over time—sometimes months, sometimes years—the name of a boyfriend is written clearly on the page, a country where I worked appears, even the plot of a show I've been working on is staring me in the face and I continue to be in awe of your gift.

By nature I am an optimist and I get the feeling that you are too. You're also very empathetic and communicate your predictions in a kind and safe atmosphere.

Thank you for your gift, your kindness and encouragement. I always leave your readings feeling uplifted, inspired and excited about the future. Knowing someone believes in you, can help you accomplish anything. And you definitely do that for me.

Much love,

Vivienne x
Glasgow, Scotland ~ August 2019

• 2 8 •

YVONNE'S STORY

East Kilbride, Scotland ~ August 2019

Hi Margaret,

THOUGHT I WOULD DROP YOU A LINE to say thank you for the readings that you have done for me. I have been blown away with the accuracy of your predictions, past and present. You truly are an inspiration and a remarkable Lady!

One of my first readings that I had, you told me that I would meet someone abroad and that you seen me travelling back and forward on a plane to visit him. I laughed this off, and thought you were mad! But, lo and behold, I met my current partner on holiday and continued traveling to see him for two years. And... he now lives in Scotland with me!

I would never have believed it until it happened—you had every detail spot on!

You also told me that the light in my car wasn't working and that I would get a new car very soon. The following week when I was in the car I had to pull off the expressway as it was losing power. To cut a long story short, you were right, my company car was replaced.

As well as all this you continue to predict marriages, babies and separations within my family and friends circle, and right to the very last detail.

You have an amazing gift Margaret, never stop what you are doing, you never disappoint.

Thanks for all your love and support.

See you soon,

Yvonne xx
East Kilbride, Scotland ~ August 2019

· 2 9 ·

NATALIE'S STORY

Scotland – June 2019

Hi Margaret,

MY ONE AND, SADLY, ONLY READING WITH YOU was done a good few years ago. But I still talk about it to this day.

When you started my reading the first person that came through was my grandad, who brought me up. You had our relationship and the type of big hard-working Irish family man he was described perfectly.

You then asked me what was happening with the passport, or the passport office, but told me not to worry that it was sorted now. I had just left the passport office for the third day in a row and got a taxi to your house for my reading straight from there. There were loads of different issues regarding my daughter's passport.

Needless to say, you were correct. The passport came a few days after my reading.

You then asked me who Jamie was. I said my partner. You then said:

"He carries all his eggs in one basket... or should that be footballs?"

My partner played football! Then you said he was going to change club soon and because of a man with black curly hair.

He signed for Aberdeen the following summer. The manager was a man called Steve Patterson and if you googled him back then, he had black curly hair.

As I was writing down everything you told me during the reading, I noticed you had a wooden sideboard in the room with a wind chime type ornament on it. And as I was writing I heard it chime, you then quickly asked me:

"Have you recently lost a baby?"

I was totally shocked at this question as no one knew I had just lost a baby, except me and my partner. I was only eight weeks pregnant. I told you yes I had, and you asked: "did you hear that chime there?" It had made a noise again. I said "yes." You then told me that was my baby letting me know it was still with me, and I would get him back when the time was right.

And yes, you guessed it... I had my baby and it was a boy. I fell pregnant 3 weeks after I got married which was when I felt the time was right. And just as you told me.

You then also asked me if I had a cyst on my right ovary. I said I don't think so. And so you told me to watch out for this during my pregnancy.

During my pregnancy I was spot bleeding so I got a scan done. The nurse told me I had a cyst on my ovary and I said let me guess... is it my right one? She said yes it is, and asked me if I'd had it a while. I said no, but Margaret Solis the psychic told me I had it. She took your number from me right there and then so she could call to book a reading with you... lol !

You told me my son would have a better left foot than his dad (yes my son also plays football). He's a left footer like his dad.

You told me I would eventually pass my driving test as I'd failed three times. I passed the fourth time.

You told me the number 28 would be important to me—I got married on the 28th May.

You also mentioned the number 14 was significant. My son was born on the 14th March.

There was so much more you told me, but sadly I lost my notes with the rest of your predictions on it. But hopefully I'll get another reading in the future from you. And soon!

Natalie x
Scotland ~ June 2019

• 3 0 •

TONY M'S STORY

Scotland ~ July 2019

Hi Lady Margaret,

I WANTED TO WRITE YOU A WEE LETTER TO THANK YOU for the time that you have spent with me during our readings. I have enjoyed our chat and banter with joy.

You have an amazing approach and manner, which automatically puts me at ease. Your gift is beyond belief. Before a reading I always feel apprehensive and slightly worried. That goes right 'oot the window from the moment we meet. I have had the honour and pleasure of knowing you for many years now given the many readings and will always hold that with fondness and admiration.

You have given a no nonsense, sensitive and humorous approach during the readings. The many insights into my personal and professional life have been spot on. So many names, births, deaths celebrations and events have all come true. Historical facts, time periods and descriptions of various things again have been spot on.

Professionally, I made a return after over 30 years to a craft that I enjoyed, yet gave up to concentrate on my family. It was during one of our readings you told me that I would be thinking about something I enjoyed when I was twenty five years of age and that I would return to that field. I have indeed done that and have been a busy wee bee acting in award-winning films, theatre, radio and television.

Now, I never saw that coming, but you did!

There are many other things that have transpired, and many yet to transpire of that I am sure.

I very much look forward to seeing you very soon for another wee reading. Not only are you incredibly gifted, your are an amazing individual. I was going to say one in a trillion but actually there is only one, regardless of numbers and that I am happy to say is you!

Thank You, Lots of Love,

Tony Macdonald, Actor
Scotland ~ July 2019

If you enjoyed reading **Secret Psychic Stories** please consider leaving a review of the book online, and on your reading platform of choice, such as Amazon.

And, please feel free to pass on this print copy of the book to someone you think would enjoy reading it.

Love and positive energy...

Margaret X

MARGARET SOLIS

A FEW WORDS
FROM MARGARET

Thank you for reading SECRET PSYCHIC STORIES: VOLUME 1. I hope you enjoyed this **prequel** to the *StarBright Series*.

As you'll possibly know from reading my books and my personal story, Huntington's disease and Cancer have been a big part of my life—with Huntington's affecting a large part of my mother's side of the family.

A cruel genetic disease, Huntington's affects muscle coordination, eventually leading to cognitive decline and dementia, followed tragically by certain death.

And having personally battled with breast cancer, I can say that doing any little bit to help in the fight against this horrid disease is also very important to me.

If you've bought this book then you will also have made a contribution in helping a good cause, or two, as I'm giving 10% of all profits made from the sale of this book to four charities—charities that aim to eradicate and alleviate the effects of both Huntington's disease and cancer from this world.

Each charity will receive 2.5% of profits.
The four charities being:

- *Scottish Huntington's Association*
- *The International Huntington's Association*
- *Cancer Research UK*
- *Macmillan Cancer Support*

If you haven't bought the book and you'd like to support these charities, as well as myself as an author, then go to Amazon and all good e-retailers and buy your copy there.

Thank you for *your* support.

Margaret X

BOOKS
BY MARGARET

The *StarBright Series:*

PREQUEL:
secret psychic stories ~ volume 1

BOOK ONE:
the good gift ~ a memoir
(coming soon)

Margaret Solis

Book One

in the

STARBRIGHT SERIES:

THE GOOD GIFT

COMING SOON...

The good gift is the remarkable breakthrough memoir about a young girl with an extraordinary ability and her journey towards becoming one of the world's top psychics and mediums.

At the age of 3 Margaret Solis has a face-to-face conversation with her Scottish grandmother. This may not seem out of the ordinary in itself, but her grandmother has been dead for 5 years.

As she gets older, Margaret struggles more and more with an ability that seems to continually grow in power and strength. In an attempt to live the 'normal' life of a teenager, and a young woman, she tries to ignore and suppress her psychic visions. This is easier thought than done however, as she gradually comes to understand the truth and that the gift is not something you can simply just switch off.

The good gift is a memoir with a difference. At its heart, it is an intimate and revealing account of the struggle for self-discovery. Yet it is also much more; a spiritual coming-of-age tale of family bonds, of love and romance, of loss and grief, of eternal friendships, of old traditions and new beginnings.

With amazing insight Margaret gives an inspiring, revealing, and sometimes dark and unbelievable account of living and coping with an unusual gift. Pulling back a veil of secrets, this biography uncovers the power of personal transformation and the inevitability and magic of destiny and how it impacts our lives.

* * *

BOOK ONE in the *StarBright Series* ~ **the good gift** ~ is coming soon to Amazon and all good book e-retailers.

$$* \quad * \quad *$$

And, as a thank you for reading **this prequel** to the *StarBright Series*—SECRET PSYCHIC STORIES: VOLUME 1, the following pages contain the first three chapters from Margaret's NEW book—*the good gift...*

1

The Black Isle

AS WE MADE OUR WAY OVER THE KESSOCK BRIDGE TOWARDS THE BLACK ISLE on that crisp, cold, November morning, we could see that it was covered in a thick, cold mist.

This was my first return to the Isle since my last visit thirty-two years before. Then, I had been just thirteen years old.

As our car drew closer to the place where my grandmother was born—a small, picture-postcard, Scottish coastal village called Avoch, I could now feel my psychic senses starting to spring to life.

The hairs on my arms and the back of my neck were suddenly standing on end, along with the goosebumps that were coursing through my whole body. Completely aware of myself, I instantly began to experience that unmistakable feeling of a familiar electricity and energy that always accompanies my transition into a heightened psychic state. This was all telling me there was a palpable energy in the air. A special energy.

I knew I would begin to see things. Things that others could not see. Things that seem strange and unbelievable to most people, but natural to me.

Accompanied on this visit to the Isle by a photographer and a journalist from one of Scotland's most popular newspapers—The Sunday Mail—I had recently been offered the position of resident psychic by the editorial team at the newspaper. If I agreed, I would be inheriting the mantle from the wonderful Darlinda, who had written for them for over twenty years.

Sadly, she'd passed away a few months earlier. A first rate psychic, Darlinda had been a good and kind friend to me. It was a sad day for many, the day she passed into spirit.

As one of Scotland's leading psychics, the newspaper now asked me if I would continue their featured weekly stars and horoscopes. It was a big decision for me. It would be a big step into the limelight, and I was thinking about whether I should do it, or not. The role came with a fair amount of public exposure, and being (for the most part) a very private person, I had to seriously think about how this might impact my life.

I'd already talked to the editor at the newspaper and

found out more about the role. In turn, their journalistic team asked their own questions for a possible feature article—wanting to find out more about what being a psychic entailed, and what it meant to experience my psychic '*gift*' at a personal level and on a day-to-day basis.

They wanted more of an insight and to share the story about what it means to be part of a family that, for generations, have been gifted with second sight.

And so, in search of answers, along with a reporter and a photographer from the newspaper, I travelled north from Glasgow to the Scottish Highlands. To my ancestral home. To the Black Isle, and the village of Avoch.

As the three of us arrived at the outskirts of the village, I asked for us to stop at the base of a hill that I recognised. I was sure this was the hill where, as a teenager, I had spent most of my care-free spring holiday so many years before. We all got out of the car, and as we did so, the pure and crisp Highland air assaulted our senses. And even though the thickness of the grey mist was limiting what we could see, I followed my psychic instincts and led our small group to the top of that hill. It wasn't long before we reached the summit. Eerily and on cue, the mist began to clear and the stunning views across the Moray Firth opened up before us. My companions laughed nervously, looking at me with a spooked out look on their face. A look that I have seen on many an occasion.

I had been hesitant about coming back to the Isle. I wasn't sure what to expect. Or, what would be expected of me. I knew now that I had nothing to worry about.

As the mist melted away, so did my nerves. We now stood looking out over the incredible views to the Moray Firth from that scenic Avoch hill. I felt I was home again. And, as my nerves started to ease and I relaxed, so did my two companions.

"Can I take a few shots for the feature article Margaret?" asked the photographer.

"Sure, not a problem." I answered.

And what a perfect place to do so. The camera clicked away, and as we stood in awe of the natural beauty of the Isle, they began asking me questions about my background and what my life was like being a psychic.

As I answered their questions, the journalist turned to me and said:

"Perfect, Margaret, I think we have just about everything we need for the feature."

"What a magical, breathtaking place this is."

"Yes it is." I replied.

"The energy here is very special. It is unique."

Every passing moment we were being deeply touched by the energy of that land. I could feel it. I could see it. The energy was there, and it was there in abundance. You could not help but be affected by it in a positive way, and in a way that was good for the soul.

As we made our way back down the hill, I could see that my companions had also been touched by that energy. They seemed more aware of *who* they were, *what* they were, and *why* they were. They had been touched by the natural energy of the Isle—whether they knew it or not. As was I.

Before we got back to the car, I had one of my psychic intuitions. And boy, was it strong. Immediately, I indicated to my companions to turn left and walk down towards the village.

Something had tugged at my psychic instinct, telling me to go towards the houses on Avoch's shorefront.

It had been over three decades since my last visit to Avoch—I wasn't sure where any of my family lived, or even if any of my relatives still lived here. I decided to trust my psychic instincts, this psychic 'tug', and led the way.

We passed dozens of little cottages and detached houses along the shorefront. Then, as we crossed over a small stone bridge, I knew we had arrived. As I hurried slightly ahead, I pointed out my grandmother's old house. I somehow knew that my uncle Tommy's house was also nearby. We walked six houses down, and before I realised what I was doing, I knocked on the door.

The door was opened by my second cousin Helen. Shocked to see me, and with a broad Highland accent, she excitedly shouted my name;

"Maaargaret!"

"Oh my, it is you!"

"Daaad!... It's Margaret..." she called to her dad within the house to let him know they had visitors.

Looking mightily pleased to see us, my uncle Tommy gallantly introduced himself. Then, in his own unique Highland style, promptly began to regale my companions with the history of Avoch. He wasn't two minutes into his first story, before he exclaimed:

"Margaret has the gift you know!"

"She sees those in spirit and can tell you a thing or two about your future."

Uncle Tommy then went on to inform us that my mother and grandmother were also blessed with the gift. My two companions were completely stunned. We hadn't yet managed to get a word in edgeways, or gotten around to telling my uncle and cousin the reason for our trip up to the Isle.

We enjoyed my uncle Tommy and cousin Helen's hospitality for the rest of that afternoon. As well as copious cups of tea and biscuits. We started to say our goodbyes and just as we were about to leave, I experienced a strong psychic feeling. A psychic lightning bolt. It stopped me in my tracks, but I knew what it was. My cousin and I looked at each other in such a way that I immediately knew she had Huntington's disease—there was no need for words. She could see it in my eyes. I knew what it meant. Years later, my fears would be sadly confirmed.

It had been a long day, and as we walked back to the car, we decided that we would go to a local pub in the nearby village of Fortrose for dinner. We took a seat at an old table in the middle of the pub, and just as we were about to order, I spotted an old man sitting in the corner. He winked at me, and as he did so, I laughed and said to the waitress:

"That's a cheeky wee man with the bunnet in the corner... imagine winking at me at his age!"

The photographer glanced over to where I was indicating. Looking puzzled, he asked me: "What wee man?"

The waitress quickly told us that the old man I could see was probably the old ghost of a one-time regular of the former 17th century inn and that the current pub was built on the foundations of that site. Over the centuries the ghost-like figure had been seen on occasion in and around the hotel by locals and visitors alike.

As he continued to grin the most mischievous of grins whilst sitting on, what I could tell was his most favourite old rickety chair, no one else seemed to be able to see the cheeky old man. The waitress went about her business as if it was the most normal thing in the world. I took it all in my stride and smiled to myself. I was accustomed to seeing spirit, and it was certainly nothing out of the ordinary for me. I started to glance over the dinner menu as the old man looked on, his playful grin turning into a warm smile.

My companions, on the other hand, could not believe how casually the people they had so far met on the Isle seemed to easily accept that spirits do, actually, exist.

2

Psychic genes

FROM A VERY YOUNG AGE I have always felt, experienced and seen things that could be classed as supernatural, paranormal or psychic. As a child I had no idea that most other people could not see what I could see. It all seemed very normal and natural to me, as I didn't know anything different. Basically, I have never known what not seeing what I can see is like.

What I saw and experienced would scare me at times, as not everything I could see was, by any means, all sweetness and light. Gradually, and as I got older, I began to understand that I wasn't quite like anyone else in that respect, and that having a psychic ability wasn't anything you could call *'normal.'*

It's probably best if I start the story about my gift of second sight in earnest, and at the beginning of my life, as this is where my psychic visions naturally started. It will also give you a back story about who I am and what kind of life I experienced, as well as how the psychic side of things crossed over into my everyday life.

I'll try to explain things as I felt and experienced them. Well at least as best as I can, as it's not easy to describe what I can see, feel, hear and experience.

* * *

I have known this gift from a very young age—when I was a small child and then maturing into a teenager, then on to a young adult, and later to an adult woman with more life experience behind me. I'll recount my experiences from these stages in my life and how each stage made me see things differently. And with the benefit of hindsight, whether I was aware of what was happening to me, or not, at the time.

There won't be too much jumping around with regards to timelines, as I'll try to keep things in a linear fashion as much as I possibly can. Inevitably though, there will be some kind of crossover where a particular event or events need further explanation, or a side story is required to explain an event, or happening.

I have found it difficult at times to fully explain what I have gone through, or what I have experienced in my life. Having a psychic gift, as you can no doubt imagine, isn't a straightforward way to live your day to day life. But, in our own way, we all have our own stuff to deal with. And my attitude as to what I have to handle is to just get on with life. It's another thing to get used to. We are, all human after all.

* * *

I was born the first daughter of a third daughter in a two bedroom Glasgow tenement flat. It was the very same house that my mother was raised in.

Brought up in that house throughout most of my childhood, I was surrounded by love—the love from my mother, my father and my grandfather, and then later, alongside my little sister and brother.

My very first memory of experiencing a 'psychic vision' was when I was three years old. Sitting on my grandfather's big old oak chest, I had a very strange conversation with a friendly old woman.

I can vividly recall my mother entering the room and asking:

"Who are you talking to?"

"Your mum!" I replied.

"How do you know it's my mum?"

"She told me... and she's sitting in her special chair... the one with the wheels on it."

This may not seem strange at first. However, my

grandmother, Margaret Patience Pirie, had died two years before I was born.

I came to understand as I grew older that this had been my very first psychic vision, and, a direct connection with the world of spirit. It was an experience I will remember all my days.

Although my mother was a bit shaken at the time, she was not surprised, and would on occasion recount that very first experience with me—often saying that it was at that moment that she knew for certain I had inherited *'the gift.'*

I began to discover as I grew older that the gift of second sight was something that was very much an accepted ability within our family.

* * *

My grandmother's family came from Avoch *(pronounced Och)*, a small village situated on The Black Isle in the north of Scotland. The Isle itself is just past what is otherwise known as the capital of the Highlands—the city of Inverness—which is located at the north end of Loch Ness.

Originally called *Ardmeanach* (Gaelic *ard*, height; *maniach*, monk, from an old religious house on the wooded ridge of Mulbuie), it is said that the Black Isle derived its customary name from the fact that, since snow does not lie in winter, the promontory looks black while the surrounding country is white. However, that is only one theory amongst many of how the Black Isle got its name. I would go as far as to say that there is a more magical and much more mystical reason for it being named as such.

Despite its name, the Black Isle is not an island but a peninsula, and is surrounded on three sides by the sea—the Cromarty Firth to the north, the Beauly Firth to the south, and with the Moray Firth to the east. The northern slopes of the Isle have some of the finest views Scotland has to offer, where *Dingwall, Ben Wyvis, Fyrish* and the deepwater anchorage at *Invergordon* present spectacular scenery. To the south, *Inverness* and the *Monadhliath Mountains* can be seen with breathtaking views.

One of the true jewels of the Scottish Highlands, the Isle includes the towns of *Cromarty* and *Fortrose*, and the villages of *Culbokie, Jemimaville, Rosemarkie, Avoch, Munlochy, Tore, North Kessock* and *Muir of Ord*, as well as numerous smaller settlements, with all in all, around 12,000 people living on the Isle.

I believe the Black Isle also has a deep mystical history. To this day there are great and strong energies which are concentrated and connected to certain locations throughout the towns and the lands of the Isle's countryside— with **Fairie Glen, Clootie Well** and

Chanonry Point being the three main points of particular strong energy on the Isle.

I've been to all of them, and I can tell you that my psychic senses stand on spine-tingling end at every one of these three points. And more so than anywhere else on the Isle, and Scotland for that matter. The only other place I ever feel like this is when I visit Rosslyn Chapel on Scotland's East coast. But that has a different kind of energy. A newer, a much more 'religious' kind. If that makes sense.

One of the strongest energies I have ever personally experienced was at *Chanonry Point*, which is just outside *Fortrose*. A natural promontory that is normally windswept and exposed to the seaborn elements of the sea and its salty winds. It is said that the Brahan Seer was burned at this location for the practice of witchcraft in the 1600s. And I believe it!

I feel such a strong connection to this particular part of the Isle. I think it must be because I have an uncommon connection with the seer. And not just in the form of psychic energy, or ability. It has been said, through and within my family, that we are descendants of the Brahan Seer, on my mother's side. Whether this is true or not, I cannot verify it. Yet, somehow, deep down in my psychic genes, I know it to be true.

The Brahan Seer, known in his native Scottish Gaelic as *Coinneach Odhar,* or *Kenneth Mackenzie,* was according to legend, a predictor of the future who lived in the 17th century.

Odhar was said to have been gifted with *'the sight'* after his mother had a psychic vision with an other-worldly spirit. After helping her pass on into spirit, *Odhar's* mother asked that her son be blessed with the gift.

The next day after his mother had passed, *Odhar* found an Adder stone—a stone with a hole in the middle of it. Said to be imbued with magical and psychic properties, *Odhar* used this stone from that day forth to focus his visions and foretell the future. And, it is said, with uncanny accuracy.

Born in the early 17th century in Uig, on the island of Lewis (situated on a chain of islands to the west of Scotland's northern coast), *Odhar* has often been compared to Nostradamus. There is a fantastic book by author *Elizabeth Sutherland* called **Ravens and Black Rain**, which goes into much detail about *Odhar*, his prophecies, and also the story of Highland second sight—I highly recommend it.

Odhar is said to have been born on lands owned by the Seaforths, and also part of the Clan Mackenzie. Having become famous as an accurate diviner and wit, he was invited to Seaforth territory in the east, to work as a labourer at Brahan Castle near Dingwall on the Black Isle. He is also said to have used his Adder stone and his power of prophecy to aid Kenneth Mackenzie, 3rd Earl of Seaforth for most of his life. Yet this line of work was to eventually be his downfall and undoing.

Famed for his psychic powers, the Countess of Seaforth, (said to be one of the ugliest women in Scotland), one day asked *Odhar* for news about her husband, the Earl, who was in France at the time. *Odhar's* response seemed to suggest that the Earl was being unfaithful to his wife with a woman that was much, much fairer than she.

At this news the Countess flew into a rage and ordered that *Odhar* be burnt to death at the nearby *Chanonry Point.*

Before he died, however, *Odhar* predicted that the heirs and the line of Seaforth Mackenzies were all doomed to extinction. This final prophecy indeed came to pass in 1815 when Francis Mackenzie, descendant of the Earl and the Countess, died. He left no sons or daughters, and the line of Mackenzies was no more.

Quite a few of *Odhar's* psychic and prophetic visions were to come true in the years following his death. These include:

The Battle of Culloden (1745), on which his words were recorded as being said at the site, 100 years before the battle: *"Oh! Drumossie, thy bleak moor shall, ere many generations have passed away, be stained with the best blood of the Highlands. Glad am I that I will not see the day, for it* *will be a fearful period; heads will be lopped off by the score, and no mercy shall be shown or quarter given on either side."*

Trains in the Highlands: *Odhar* talked of great black horse-like beasts, belching fire and steam, and drawing many carriages through the glens, saying *"I would not like to live when a black bridleless horse shall pass through the Muir of Ord."* Railways were built through the Highlands more than 200 years later. Trains, of course, were to be those black bridleless horses.

The joining of the lochs in the Great Glen: In 1620 *Odhar* predicted that full-rigged ships would one day be sailing round the back of Tomnahurick, near Inverness, at a time when the only navigable route near the location was the River Ness, on the other side of Tomnahurick. Connecting the Scottish east coast at Inverness with the west coast at Corpach near Fort William in Scotland, the Caledonian Canal was constructed in the early nineteenth century by Scottish engineer Thomas Telford.

The Scottish Parliament would once again reopen: *Odhar* spoke of the day when Scotland would once more have its own Parliament. This would come, he said, when *"men could walk dry shod from England to France."* The Channel Tunnel opened in 1994. A few years later the Scottish Parliament was established and opened—the first since 1707.

Odhar foretold North Sea oil: "A black rain will bring

riches to Aberdeen." Aberdeen has indeed prospered and flourished from the discovery of plentiful black gold *(oil)* in the North Sea.

Pointing to a field far from the shore, he said that a ship would anchor there one day. *"A village with four churches will get another spire,"* said *Odhar, "and a ship will come from the sky and moor at it."* Strangely, this actually happened in 1932 when an airship made an emergency landing and was 'moored' and tied up to the spire of the village's new church.

The prophecy of a great flood. Clach an Tiompain (the *'Sounding Stone'*) or *'The Eagle Stone'* is a small Pictish stone, around 80cm tall, located on a hill on the northern outskirts of Strathpeffer in Easter Ross, Scotland. The stone was originally located further down the hill, towards Dingwall, but was moved to its current site in 1411.

One old tradition is that the stone marks the site of a Scottish clan battle that took place in 1411 between the Clan Munro and a branch of the Clan MacDonald, and that the stone commemorates a Munro victory as it is marked with their symbol—an eagle.

The stone is also associated with the prophecies of *Odhar;* he predicted that if the stone fell three times, the surrounding valley would be flooded, and the stone used as an anchor. It has since fallen twice, and when it fell for the second time, the Cromarty Firth rose up and flooded the neighbouring town of Dingwall.

The eagle stone is now set in concrete!

* * *

Whether my family is connected to *Coinneach Odhar, the Brahan Seer,* is really of no consequence. In essence, it means nothing whether I am or not.

What I do know is that I feel certain abnormally strong psychic energies with every one of my visits to the Black Isle. Whether this is connected to *Odhar* I cannot be sure.

But what I know to be true is that my psychic energy is re-energised with every visit to Avoch and the Isle. I use this energy to do as much good as I can, and that good mostly comes in the form that I know best—where I help people that come to me in need of guidance, or in wanting to know what their future holds. And in my experience these two things are, more often than not, found to be one and the same.

3

Grandpa Fergus,
fairies
and magic

MY UPBRINGING AS A CHILD WAS TYPICAL OF A GLASGOW FAMILY— lots of laughs, buckets full of love, but very little money. I was a child of the 1950s, and in those post-war years, things were straightforward; people appreciated the simple things in life and made do with what they had. Neighbours were like family too, where communities stuck together and looked out for each other.

Throughout my early years, there was one man who became my idol—my wonderful grandfather.

Fergus McAndrew Pirie was born and raised

in beautiful Banff—a small town north and west of Scotland's major oil town of Aberdeen, the granite city. A grandfather on my mum's side, his surname Pirie aptly derives from the French diminutive of Peter, which means 'The Rock.'

'Grandpa Fergus' as I affectionately called him, played a huge role in my life, teaching me to read and write long before I started school. He was my hero and also *my* rock. Certainly living up to his name many times over, he was always there whenever I was most in need of him.

Starting school for me was at first somewhat traumatic, as it is for some children. A very shy and introverted child, I just didn't like to leave the safety and comfort of my own family home. People that know me now can't imagine me being like that at all. But please believe me when I say that I was a quiet, wee, shy soul... once upon a time.

I remember going to school around an early age of four. Being born in March meant that way back then in the 1950s, and having a different system in place, I was enrolled and basically became the youngest child in that year, and also the class.

From the age of five, my Grandpa Fergus would get me up around 7.45am every morning, school day or not. My duty before we all had breakfast was to go across the road to the shops for milk and bread. By the time I got back from my morning errand he would have a lovely bowl of steaming hot porridge waiting for me and my younger sister, Susan, on the breakfast table.

But little did Grandpa Fergus know (or so we liked to tell ourselves) that we would always sneak a little bit of sugar into our porridge bowls. Whether he actually knew what we did or not, I will never have the privilege of knowing, but I'm sure he laughed at our antics all the same.

Now, the old traditional Scots way to eat your porridge is with salt and water. And take it from me, Grandpa Fergus was a very traditional Scots grandfather. So I guess us putting sugar in our porridge would be like putting water in your whisky to him—another custom at which he was also horrified at.

As Grandpa Fergus would watch us, we ate up every morsel of our sweet porridge. Then, and only then, were we ready in his eyes to take on whatever that day would bring us.

* * *

As far back as I can remember I have believed in fairies, spirits, and other things which to me, seemed magical, enchanting, and by their very existence, self-evident.

As a young girl and growing up through my early

teens I shared a bedroom with my younger sister, Susan. Whether it was a sunny day, or not, our bedroom would always have a vibrant, bright and glowing shaft of light that flooded in through its window and lit up the room. Some days this light was more intense than on others. Yet strangely, the intenseness had nothing to do with the actual shaft of sunlight, or moonlight.

I was mesmerized by this ray of light and would spend hours staring at it, not wanting to leave the room for anything. It fascinated me. And once I started looking into its enchanting depths, it wouldn't be long before I would start to see things dancing in the light.

At first these seemed like little dust particles. However, these particles transformed into small fairy-like figures. They would clump together and swarm—much like birds and fish do. Or, they would sometimes dance aloof and all by themselves in a defiant manner. When they were together they danced a joyful dance. Apart, not so much. It all seemed so very magical to me, and I was truly spellbound by these energetic little *fairies.*

Sitting on Grandpa Fergus's old oak chest and staring intently at that magical ray of light, I would also sometimes begin to see faces. From children, to adult, to older folk—I would see faces of all ages. I somehow knew these were spirits. I don't know how I knew, I just did. They didn't say anything, or even try to talk to me in any way, they would just appear and disappear. Fading in and out of my perception. They were friendly faces, and would often smile at me as I stared at them. I, in turn, smiled back with wide-eyed wonder.

Susan would sit with me sometimes, and she said she could also see a few of the fairies, and even the faces. But they didn't captivate her as much as they did me. Maybe she couldn't see as much as I did? Or possibly they didn't hold her attention. She preferred to go out and play with her friends, rather than sit for hours on end—*fairy-gazing*—as we called it.

* * *

BOOK ONE in the *StarBright Series* ~ ***the good gift*** ~ coming soon to Amazon and all good e-retailers.

To keep up-to-date with the release of the book subscribe to Margaret's *V.I.P. Stars Club* email Newsletter at ***www.margaretsolis.com***

By signing up you'll also gain access to weekly Star Sign Predictions sent straight to your inbox... PLUS... You'll receive exclusive content, as well as latest News, Book Updates and Special Offers.

Margaret Solis

GET EXCLUSIVE V.I.P. CONTENT

★ ★ ★ ★ ★

Building a relationship with my readers and clients is one of the very best things about sharing and writing what I have experienced day-to-day, over the course of my psychic life.

Email is a great way for me to stay in touch with you and build this friendship. So if you'd like to hear more from me, then join my *V.I.P. Stars Club email newsletter* for access to weekly Star Sign Predictions sent straight to your inbox... PLUS... You'll receive exclusive content, as well as my latest *News, Book Updates* and *Special Offers.*

Join my *V.I.P. Stars Club* with your email on my website: **www.margaretsolis.com**

Margaret X

★ ★ ★ ★ ★

Printed in Great Britain
by Amazon

29986952R00078